DATE DUE

			⟵

READING POWER

Extreme Machines

Low Riders

Scott P. Werther

The Rosen Publishing Group's
PowerKids Press™
New York

Published in 2002 by The Rosen Publishing Group, Inc.
29 East 21st Street, New York, NY 10010

First Edition

Book Design: Michelle Innes

Photo Credits: © Jack Parsons

Werther, Scott P.
Low riders / by Scott P. Werther.
   p. cm. – (Extreme machines)
Includes bibliographical references and index.
ISBN 0-8239-5954-6 (library binding)
1. Lowriders–Juvenile literature. [1. Lowriders. 2. Automobiles–Customizing.] I. Title.
TL255.2 .W47 2001
629.28'72–dc21

                                        2001000164

Manufactured in the United States of America

Contents

Low Riders

This is a low rider. It is
an old car that has been
made low to the ground.

This low rider is a car
from 1963.

This low rider is very long.

This low rider is very old.

Inside and Outside

This is the inside of a low rider.

Some low riders have fancy paint jobs like this one.

Special Lifts

This low rider has lifts at the wheels that make the front and the back of the car go up and down. The back of this low rider is down.

The back of this low rider is up.

Low riders can also be trucks.
This low rider truck has gold
flames on the side.

Glossary

fancy (**fan**-see) something that is made
   to look nice

flame (**flaym**) the part of a fire that you can
   see shoot up into the air

lift (**lihft**) something that makes things go
   up and down

low rider (**loh ry**-duhr) a car that is made to
   be close to the ground

Resources

Books

Eyewitness: Car
by Richard Sutton, Dave King, Mike Dunning
Dorling Kindersley Publishing (2000)

Classic American Cars
by Quentin Willson, Matthew Ward
Dorling Kindersley Publishing (1997)

Index

Word Count: 110

Note to Librarians, Teachers, and Parents

If reading is a challenge, Reading Power is a solution! Reading Power is perfect for readers who want high-interest subject matter at an accessible reading level. These fact-filled, photo-illustrated books are designed for readers who want straightforward vocabulary, engaging topics, and a manageable reading experience. With clear picture/text correspondence, leveled Reading Power books put the reader in charge. Now readers have the power to get the information they want and the skills they need in a user-friendly format.